MW01340753

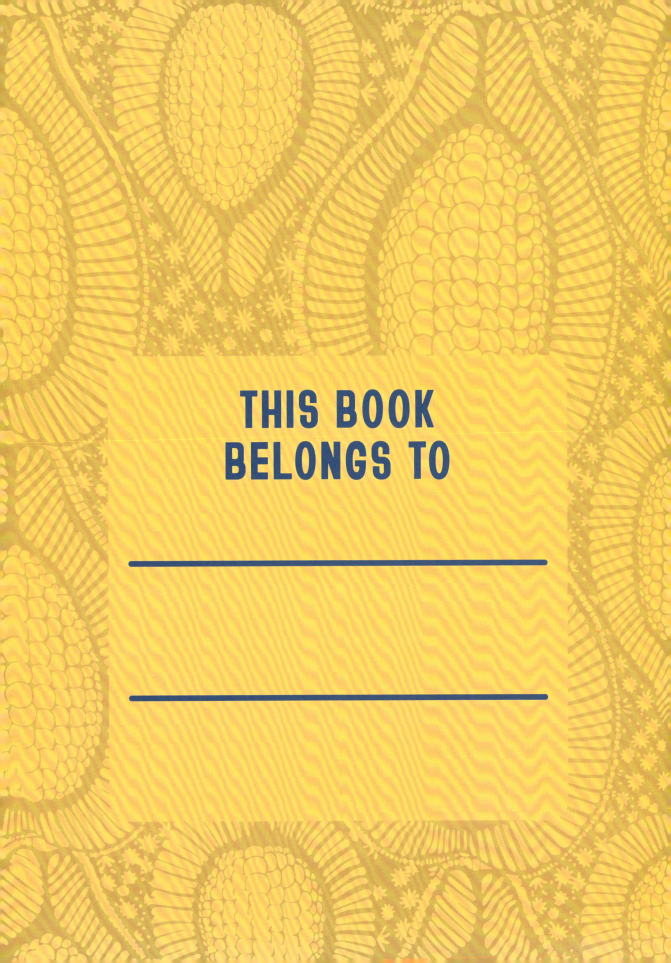

Copyright © 2021 by *B is for Black Black Brilliance*, LLC

B is for Black Black Brilliance believes that copyrights acknowledge and give credit to the hard work of individual creators. Thank you for purchasing a copy of our book and for complying with copyright expectations. Please ask permission before reproducing, scanning, or sharing any part of this book. This will help us continue to create high quality content that acknowledges, cultivates, and celebrates Black brilliance.

B is for Black Brilliance is a registered trademark.

B is for Black Brilliance is available in large quantities and welcomes the opportunity to support schools, libraries, and other organizations as they commit to supporting Black brilliance and Black futures. For more information, go to bisforblackbrilliance.com

This book is designed to spawn curiosity. Each page has a short passage to provoke further dialogue and research into the lives of each individual. This book is not meant to be an exhaustive account of the events in each person's life.

All rights reserved. No part of this book may be reproduced or used in any manner without written permission of the copyright owner except for the use of quotations in a book review.

ISBN: 978-1-7377234-1-7

B is for Black Brilliance, LLC
Henderson, NV

Envisioned and authored by Shawna Wells
Graphic design by Kellie Marsh (www.kdmgraphicdesign.com)
Cover design by Tami Boyce (tamiboyce.com)

For more products or bulk purchasing please visit bisforblackbrilliance.com

B IS FOR BLACK BRILLIANCE

WRITTEN BY SHAWNA WELLS
ILLUSTRATED BY KELLIE MARSH

*To my ancestors, to my daughter, to my son, and to you.
In honor of every Black and brilliant human:*

YOU CAN
YOU WILL
YOU ARE

PREFACE

This book was written and illustrated by Black creatives and is special to us for so many reasons.

We wrote and designed this book as an act of revolutionary love. As Black creatives, we were looking to find ourselves and express our brilliance. As we searched our souls during the creative process, we realized the power and vision that lies within all of us.

Our book concept was shared with hundreds of people, and we gratefully gathered input and received a tremendous amount of support along the way. We witnessed the shared energy generated by others contributions and realized the time is now for this material to be shared with the masses. We wrote it for every past, present, and future Black and brilliant human in the world.

This book and our organization are working, alongside each of you, to reclaim the narrative of Blackness and build momentum for Black mobility, wealth, and abundance for generations to come.

At *B is for Black Brilliance*, we provide opportunities for Black children to dream and for Black caregivers to heal—helping each person envision and build an abundant and liberated life, community, and world.

We are deeply grateful for our ancestors, our friends, our families, our supporters, and YOU.

Thank you for joining our movement!

Shawna Wells
B is for Black Brilliance

TABLE OF CONTENTS

Amanda Gorman 2

Bernard Harris Jr. 4

Claudette Colvin 6

Dr. Daniel Hale Williams 8

Ella Baker 10

Frederick Douglass 12

Garrett Morgan 14

Harriet Tubman 16

Issa Rae 18

James West 20

Kamala Harris 22

Leslie Odom Jr. 24

Mary Mcleod Bethune 26

Nat Turner 28

Octavia Butler 30

Paul Revere Williams 32

Queen Latifah 34

Ralph Bunche 36

"Stagecoach" Mary Fields 38

Toussaint Louverture 40

Usain Bolt 42

Vonetta Flowers 44

Whitney Ingram 46

Xernona Clayton 48

Yaa Asantewaa 50

Zora Neale Hurston 52

Meet the Author and Illustrator 55

Acknowledgements 57

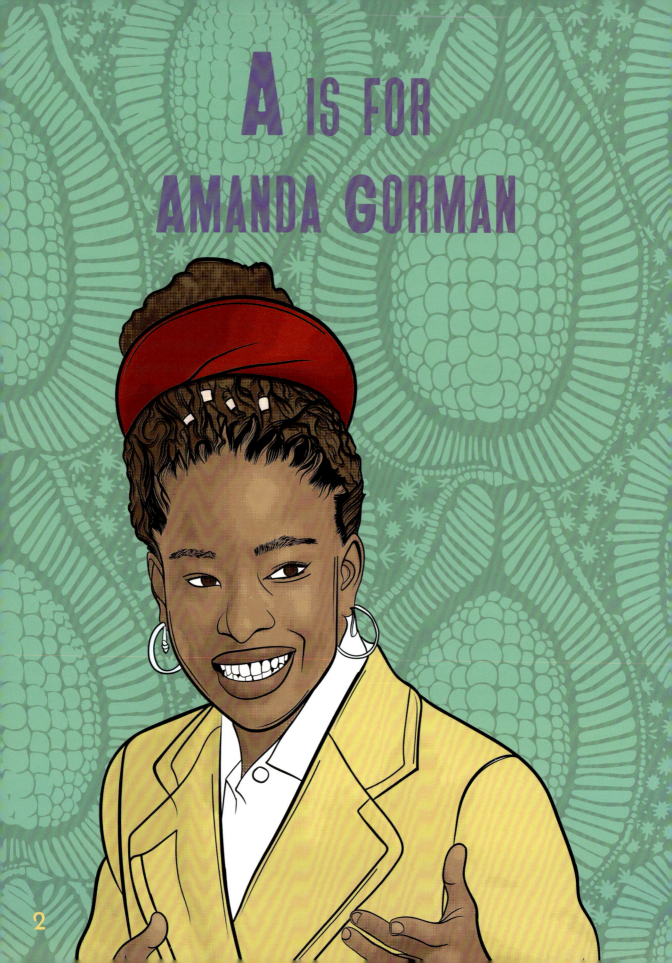

AMANDA GORMAN

POET. ACTIVIST. CAPTIVATOR.

AMANDA SHARES HER BRILLIANCE WITH US THROUGH SPOKEN AND WRITTEN WORD. SHE WRITES AND SPEAKS ABOUT RACE, SOCIAL JUSTICE, AND ENVIRONMENTAL ISSUES. SHE CAPTIVATED THE WORLD WHEN SHE SPOKE AT THE 2021 PRESIDENTIAL INAUGURATION. SHE USES HER WRITING TO SHARE IMPACTFUL MESSAGES WITH CHILDREN OF ALL AGES. AMANDA GORMAN SHARES TRUTHS, ACTIVATES HOPE, AND INSPIRES ACTION.

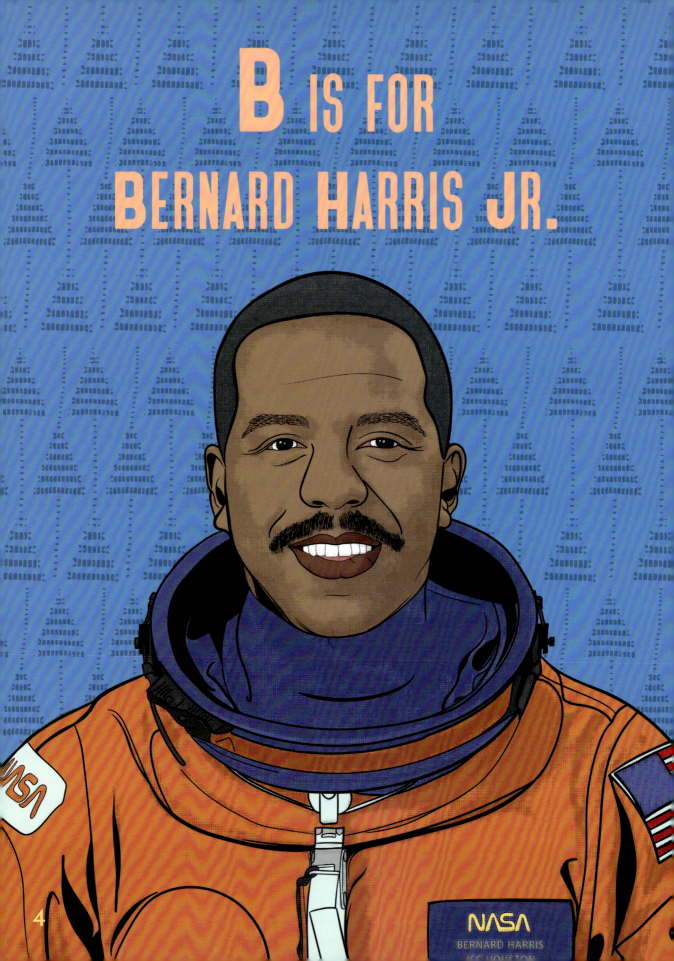

BERNARD HARRIS JR.

FLIGHT SURGEON. ASTRONAUT. PILOT.

BERNARD SHARED HIS BRILLIANCE WITH US AS A MEDICAL DOCTOR AND ASTRONAUT. BERNARD JOINED NASA AS A FLIGHT SURGEON, CLINICAL SCIENTIST, AND A CONTRIBUTOR TO THE CONSTRUCTION OF THE SPACE ROVER. BERNARD ALSO BECAME A TRAINED NASA ASTRONAUT, AND HE WAS THE FIRST BLACK MAN TO WALK ON THE MOON. HE HAS BEEN TO THE MOON TWICE AND HAS TRAVELLED OVER 7 MILLION MILES IN SPACE. BERNARD CONTINUES TO INVEST IN EMPOWERING AND SUPPORTING OTHERS TO PURSUE THEIR DREAMS.

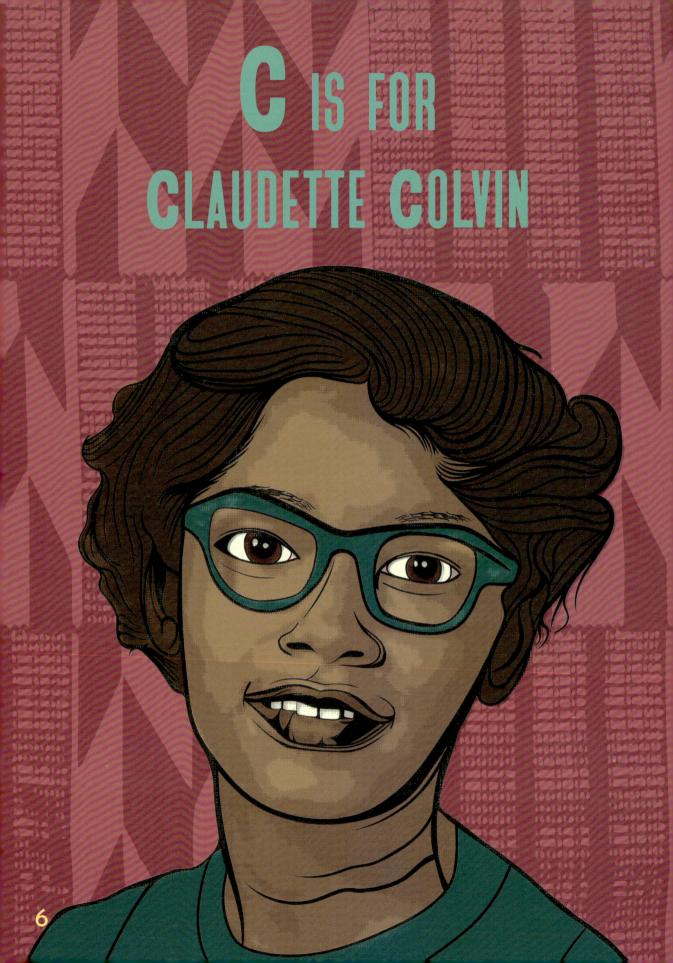

CLAUDETTE COLVIN

PROTESTOR. MOTHER. IGNITOR.

CLAUDETTE SHARED HER BRILLIANCE WITH US THROUGH RESISTANCE AND PROTEST. SHE BECAME A PIONEER OF THE 1960S CIVIL RIGHTS MOVEMENT AT JUST 15 YEARS OLD. CLAUDETTE REFUSED TO GIVE UP HER SEAT ON A CITY BUS TO A WHITE WOMAN, AND HER ACTION SPARKED THE MONTGOMERY BUS BOYCOTTS WHICH MADE HER AN INTEGRAL PART OF ENDING BUS SEGREGATION IN ALABAMA. CLAUDETTE CONTINUES TO TAKE OPPORTUNITIES TO SHARE HER STORY IN AN EFFORT TO ENCOURAGE ALL YOUNG PEOPLE TO STAND UP FOR WHAT THEY BELIEVE IN.

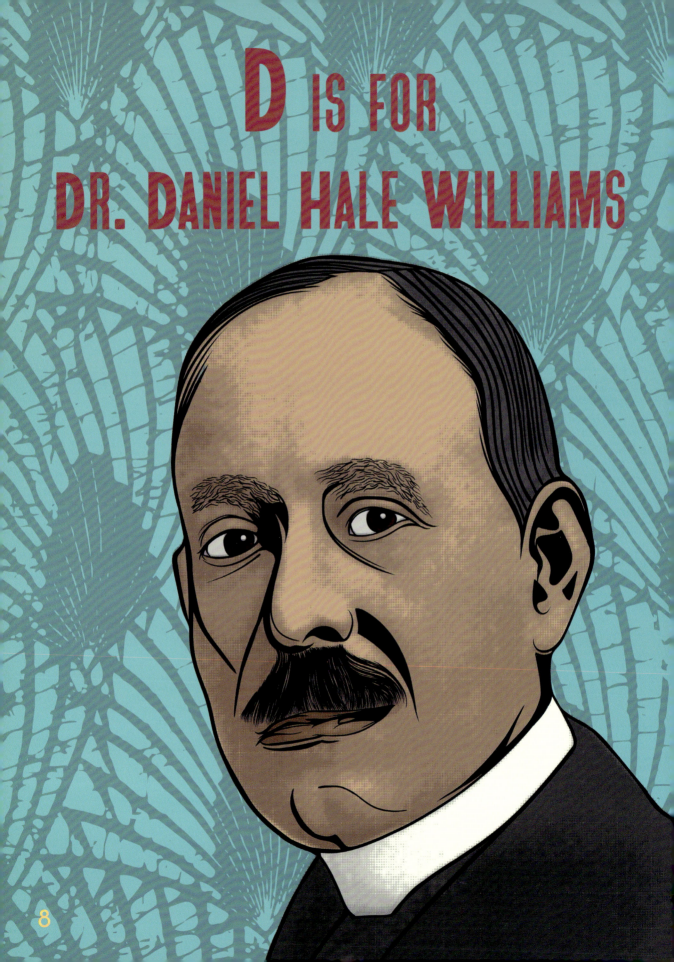

DR. DANIEL HALE WILLIAMS

SURGEON. FOUNDER. MENTOR.

DR. DANIEL SHARED HIS BRILLIANCE WITH US THROUGH MEDICINE. HE WAS THE FIRST BLACK DOCTOR TO PERFORM A SUCCESSFUL PERICARDIUM, SURGERY TO REPAIR THE HEART, IN 1893. HIS PATIENT SURVIVED THE HEART SURGERY AND LIVED FOR ANOTHER 20 YEARS. DR. DANIEL ALSO FOUNDED PROVIDENT HOSPITAL IN CHICAGO WHICH HAD A RESIDENCY PROGRAM FOR DOCTORS AND NURSES. HE WAS THE CO-FOUNDER OF THE NATIONAL MEDICAL ASSOCIATION AND A CHARTER MEMBER OF THE AMERICAN COLLEGE OF SURGEONS, WHERE HE ADVOCATED FOR THE CREATION OF MORE HOSPITALS THAT ADMITTED AND TRAINED BLACK PEOPLE. DR. DANIEL'S WORK OPENED THE DOOR FOR MANY ASPIRING BLACK DOCTORS AND NURSES.

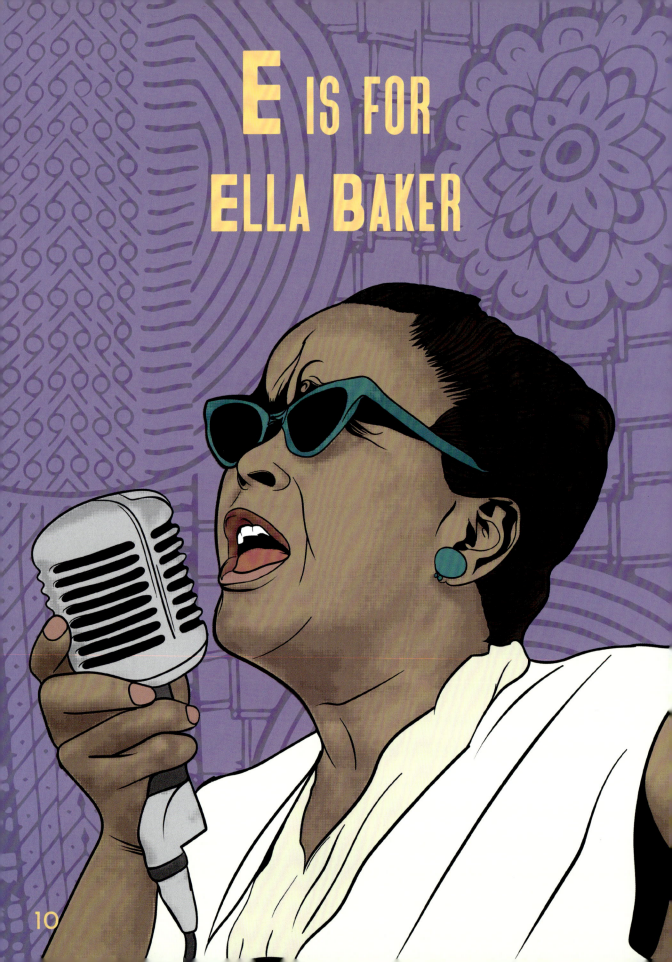

ELLA BAKER

POLITICAL ORGANIZER. GUIDE. LEGACY BUILDER.

ELLA SHARED HER BRILLIANCE WITH US THROUGH ORGANIZING AND MENTORSHIP. SHE WAS A GRASSROOTS ORGANIZER DURING THE 1960S CIVIL RIGHTS ERA WHO WORKED TO ELEVATE THE VOICES OF BLACK PEOPLE. SHE WAS A PRIMARY ADVISOR TO MANY LEADERS IN THE CIVIL RIGHTS MOVEMENT AND THE STUDENT NONVIOLENCE COORDINATING COMMITTEE (SNCC), AND SHE EVEN BECAME PRESIDENT OF THE NAACP. ELLA IS KNOWN AS ONE OF THE MOST INFLUENTIAL WOMEN OF THE CIVIL RIGHTS MOVEMENT.

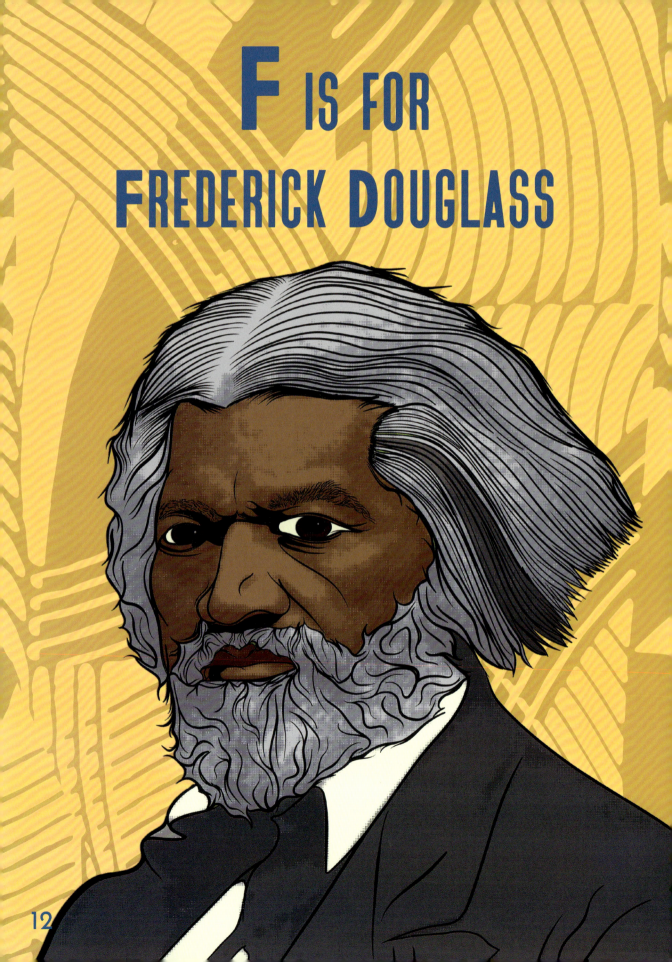

FREDERICK DOUGLASS

WRITER. ORATOR. ABOLITIONIST.

FREDERICK SHARED HIS BRILLIANCE WITH US AS A GREAT SPEAKER AND WRITER. HE WAS ALSO AN ABOLITIONIST AND SOCIAL REFORMER WHO SPOKE OUT AGAINST ENSLAVEMENT. HE URGED WHITE PEOPLE TO SEE HIM AND ALL BLACK PEOPLE AS HUMAN BEINGS. HE DEVOTED HIS TIME, ENERGY, AND TALENT TO POINT OUT RACIAL INEQUALITY TO PEOPLE IN PLACES OF POWER AND PRIVILEGE. FREDERICK DOUGLASS SERVED AS STATESMEN, AN ADVISOR TO PRESIDENTS, AND SUPPORTER OF WOMEN WHO WERE FIGHTING FOR THE RIGHT TO VOTE. FREDERICK BECAME ONE OF THE MOST NOTABLE AND INFLUENTIAL BLACK AMERICANS OF HIS TIME. HIS ACTIVISM PAVED THE WAY FOR MOVEMENTS SUCH AS THE 1960S CIVIL RIGHTS MOVEMENT AND THE PRESENT DAY BLACK LIVES MATTER MOVEMENT.

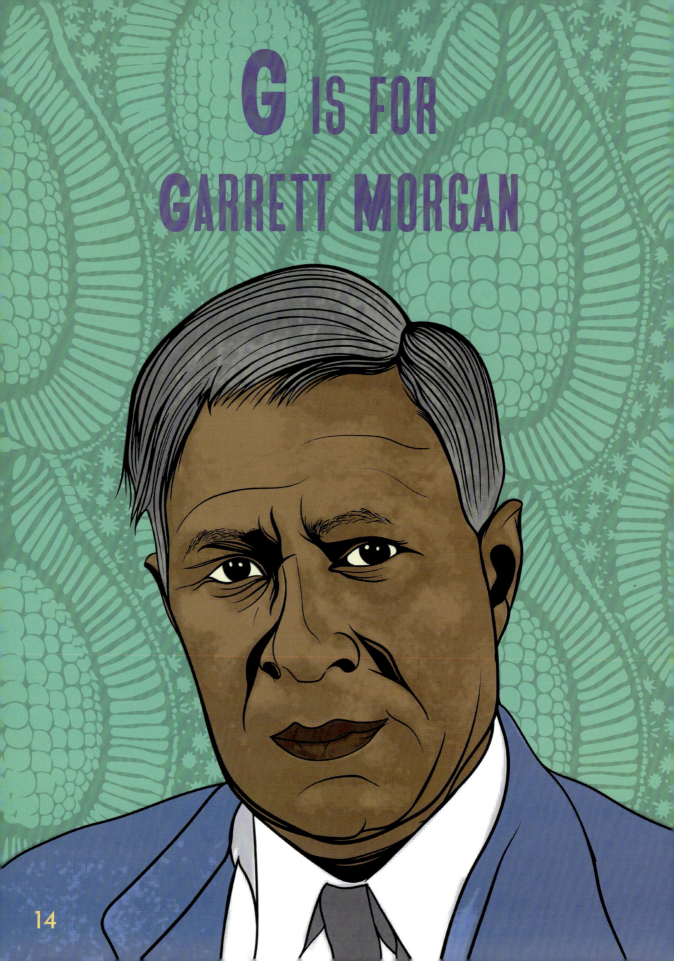

GARRETT MORGAN

INVENTOR. CREATOR. PROBLEM SOLVER.

GARRETT SHARED HIS BRILLIANCE WITH US THROUGH INVENTION. HE DEVELOPED THE THREE-POSITION TRAFFIC LIGHT, A BREATHING DEVICE, AND A CHEMICAL HAIR STRAIGHTENING SOLUTION. HIS INVENTIONS WERE DESIGNED TO MAKE LIFE BETTER, SAFER, AND MORE EFFICIENT. THE BREATHING MACHINE HE INVENTED SAVED 2 PEOPLE WHO WERE CAUGHT IN A NATURAL GAS EXPLOSION. HE ALSO PUBLISHED HIS OWN NEWSPAPER AND WORKED TO CREATE SPACES FOR BLACK JOY AND CONNECTION. GARRETT'S TENDENCY TO TINKER AND INVENT CHANGED THE WAY WE MOVE THROUGHOUT THE WORLD.

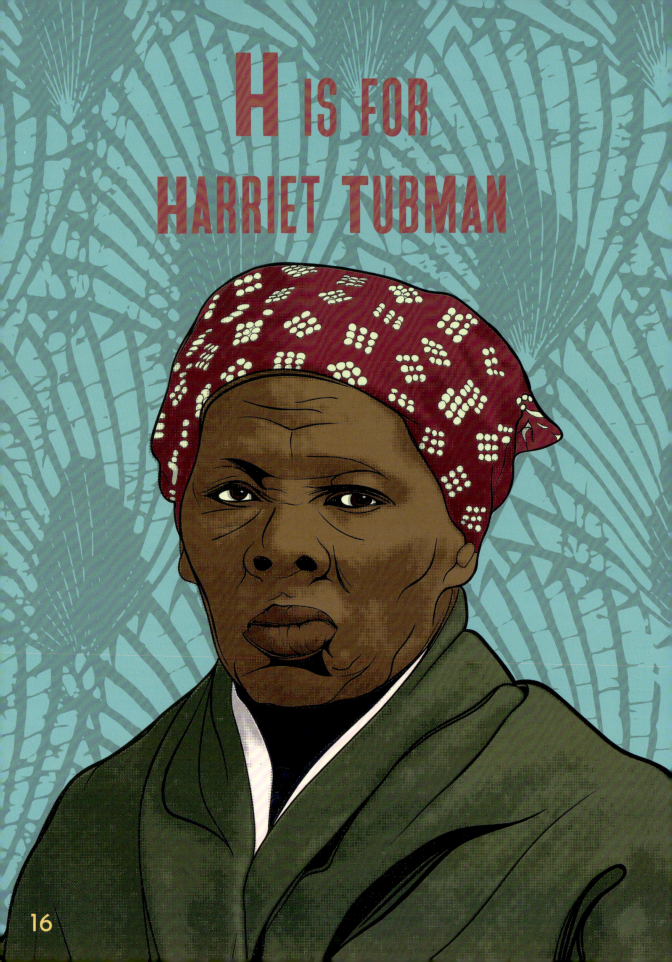

HARRIET TUBMAN

RAID LEADER. PATHFINDER. SUFFRAGETTE.

HARRIET SHARED HER BRILLIANCE WITH US THROUGH PURSUING FREEDOM FOR HERSELF AND OTHERS. HARRIET USED THE UNDERGROUND RAILROAD AND HELPED OVER 70 ENSLAVED PEOPLE FIND FREEDOM, AND SHE ALSO BECAME FREE. AS AN ABOLITIONIST, POLITICAL ACTIVIST, SPY, RAID LEADER, AND WOMAN SEEKING VOTING RIGHTS, HARRIET TUBMAN SPENT HER DAYS FIGHTING FOR A BETTER QUALITY OF LIFE FOR BLACK PEOPLE AND THE ELDERLY. HARRIET STILL REMAINS ONE OF THE MOST POWERFUL WOMEN OF HER TIME, AND PRESIDENTS HAVE CONSIDERED MAKING HER THE FACE OF THE $20 BILL .

ISSA RAE

YOUTUBER. ACTRESS. PRODUCER.

ISSA RAE SHARES HER BRILLIANCE WITH US THROUGH WRITING, ACTING, AND PRODUCING TELEVISION. HER TV SHOWS, MOVIES, AND SHORT FILMS HIGHLIGHT THE EXPERIENCES OF BLACK PEOPLE IN EVERYDAY LIFE. ISSA RAE'S CAREER WAS LAUNCHED THROUGH A POPULAR YOUTUBE SERIES THAT SHE CREATED. IN 2018 ISSA WAS NAMED ONE OF THE MOST INFLUENTIAL PEOPLE IN THE WORLD, AND SHE HAS BECOME AN AWARD-WINNING AUTHOR AND ACTRESS WHO CONTINUES TO INSPIRE THE WORLD WITH HER CREATIVITY.

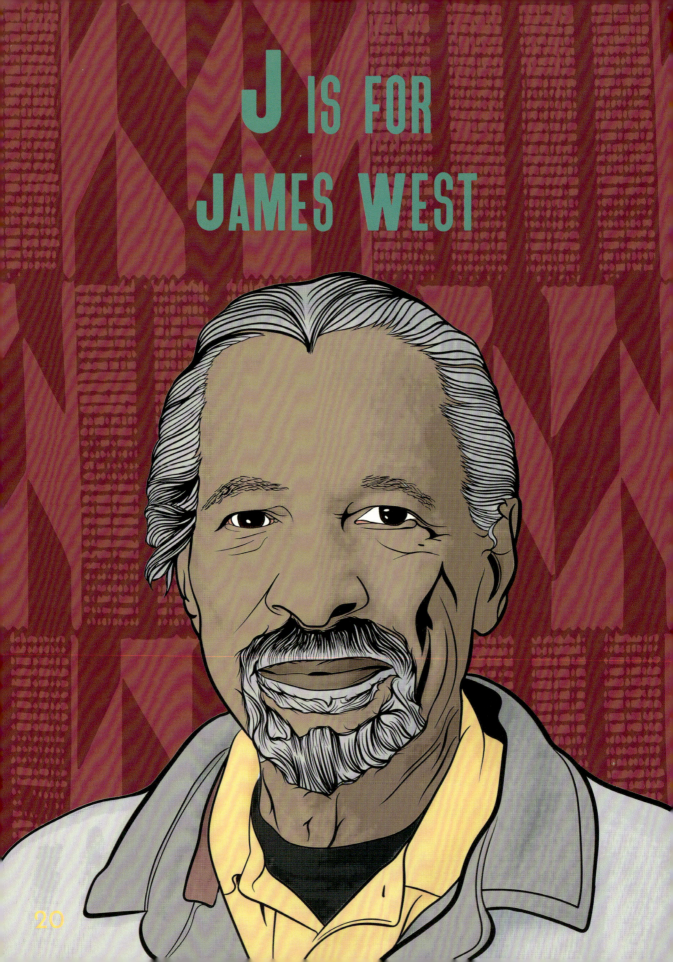

JAMES WEST

ADVOCATE. PRODIGY. TEACHER.

JAMES SHARES HIS BRILLIANCE WITH US THROUGH SOUND AND INNOVATION. HE CREATED THE MICROPHONE TECHNOLOGY WE USE IN CELL PHONES, HEARING AIDS, AND BABY MONITORS. JAMES HOLDS OVER 250 PATENTS FOR HIS INVENTIONS. HIS WORK HAS GIVEN US THE GIFT OF SOUND IN MANY DEVICES THAT WE STILL USE. IN ADDITION TO HIS CONTRIBUTIONS AS AN INVENTOR, JAMES IS AN ACTIVE CHANGE MAKER AND ADVOCATE FOR DIVERSITY IN THE FIELDS OF MATH AND SCIENCE.

KAMALA HARRIS

PRINCIPLED. TRAILBLAZER. VICE PRESIDENT.

KAMALA SHARES HER BRILLIANCE WITH US THROUGH ADVOCACY AND LEADERSHIP. SHE BEGAN PRACTICING LAW AT THE DISTRICT ATTORNEY OFFICES IN THE SAN FRANCISCO AREA. DURING HER LAW CAREER, SHE LEARNED THE IMPORTANCE OF PROTECTING THE RIGHTS OF AMERICAN PEOPLE. SHE LATER RAN FOR SENATE AND BECAME THE SECOND BLACK-AMERICAN AND FIRST ASIAN-AMERICAN SENATOR. HER WORK AS SENATOR LED HER TO RUN FOR PRESIDENT AND SHE ULTIMATELY BECAME THE VICE PRESIDENT OF THE UNITED STATES OF AMERICA. SHE IS NOW THE FIRST BLACK AND ASIAN VICE PRESIDENT OF THE UNITED STATES. KAMALA INVESTS TIME IN INSTILLING A MESSAGE OF HOPE TO EVERYONE SHE MEETS—ESPECIALLY CHILDREN.

LESLIE ODOM JR.

BROADWAY PERFORMER.
BRIDGING ANCESTOR. SINGER.

LESLIE SHARES HIS BRILLIANCE WITH US THROUGH ACTING AND SINGING. HE PURSUED HIS PASSION FOR PERFORMING BY BECOMING A CAST MEMBER IN THE BROADWAY MUSICAL "RENT" AT THE AGE OF 17. HE WORKED HARD ON HIS CRAFT AND HAS STARRED IN SEVERAL BROADWAY AND OFF-BROADWAY MUSICALS INCLUDING "TICK TICK BOOM" AND "HAMILTON." HIS ROLES HAVE BROUGHT SEVERAL BLACK HISTORICAL FIGURES TO LIFE, AND HIS PERFORMANCES HAVE LED HIM TO GAIN MANY ACCOLADES AND AWARDS. LESLIE'S BODY OF WORK CONTINUES TO HAVE CULTURAL INFLUENCE, AND HIS STORIED CAREER MOTIVATES YOUNG ENTERTAINERS TO PASSIONATELY PURSUE THEATER.

MARY MCLEOD BETHUNE

EDUCATOR. SISTER. PHILANTHROPIST.

MARY SHARED HER BRILLIANCE WITH US THROUGH EDUCATION AND PHILANTHROPY. SHE MADE THE CHOICE TO ATTEND TRINITY MISSION SCHOOL, A ONE-ROOM SCHOOLHOUSE, TO LEARN TO READ. SHE WAS THE ONLY PERSON IN HER FAMILY WHO WAS ABLE TO GO TO SCHOOL, AND AFTER SCHOOL SHE TAUGHT EVERYONE IN HER FAMILY WHAT SHE'D LEARNED. SHE SAW FIRSTHAND THE POWER OF EDUCATION AND DECIDED TO BUILD, FOUND, AND LEAD A SCHOOL TO EDUCATE AND EMPOWER YOUNG GIRLS. IN ADDITION TO RUNNING THE SCHOOL, SHE BECAME AN ADVISOR TO PRESIDENT FRANKLIN D. ROOSEVELT AND A FIERCE ADVOCATE FOR THE CIVIL RIGHTS OF BLACK WOMEN—MOST SIGNIFICANTLY FIGHTING FOR THEIR RIGHT TO VOTE. MARY BELIEVED THAT BLACK BUSINESS OWNERSHIP AND SELF-SUFFICIENCY WERE THE KEY TO BUILDING POWER AND WEALTH IN THE BLACK COMMUNITY. MARY'S IDEAS AND GROUNDWORK STILL PROVIDE US WITH A BLUEPRINT FOR BLACK EMPOWERMENT.

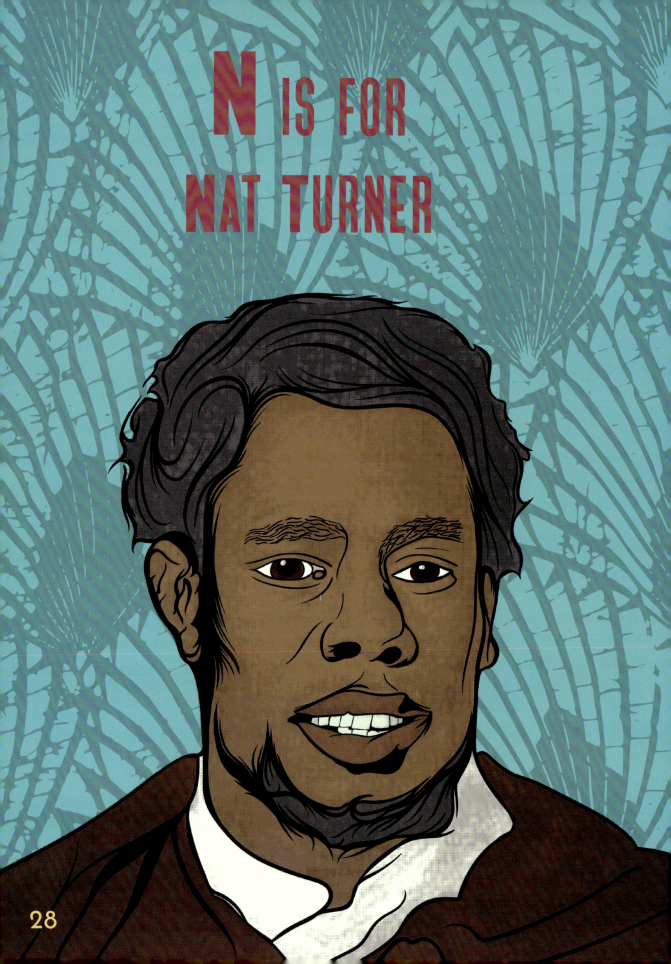

NAT TURNER

PREACHER. STRATEGIST. REVOLUTIONARY.

NAT SHARED HIS BRILLIANCE WITH US THROUGH PREACHING AND CHALLENGING THE STATUS QUO. NAT WAS BORN INTO ENSLAVEMENT, BUT HE LEARNED HOW TO READ AND WRITE AS A YOUNG BOY. NAT'S ABILITY TO READ AND WRITE HELPED HIM TO MEMORIZE SCRIPTURE AND HE LATER BECAME A PREACHER. AS HE PREACHED, HE DEVELOPED A BELIEF THAT HE HAD A GREATER PURPOSE AND HE ORGANIZED A REBELLION TO HELP FREE OTHER ENSLAVED PEOPLE. NAT'S DESIRE FOR CHANGE TOOK A LOT OF PLANNING AND COURAGE. WHILE HIS REBELLION DID NOT PRODUCE HIS DESIRED OUTCOME, NAT TURNER'S REBELLION IS SAID TO BE ONE OF THE FIRST EVENTS THAT LED TO THE AMERICAN CIVIL WAR.

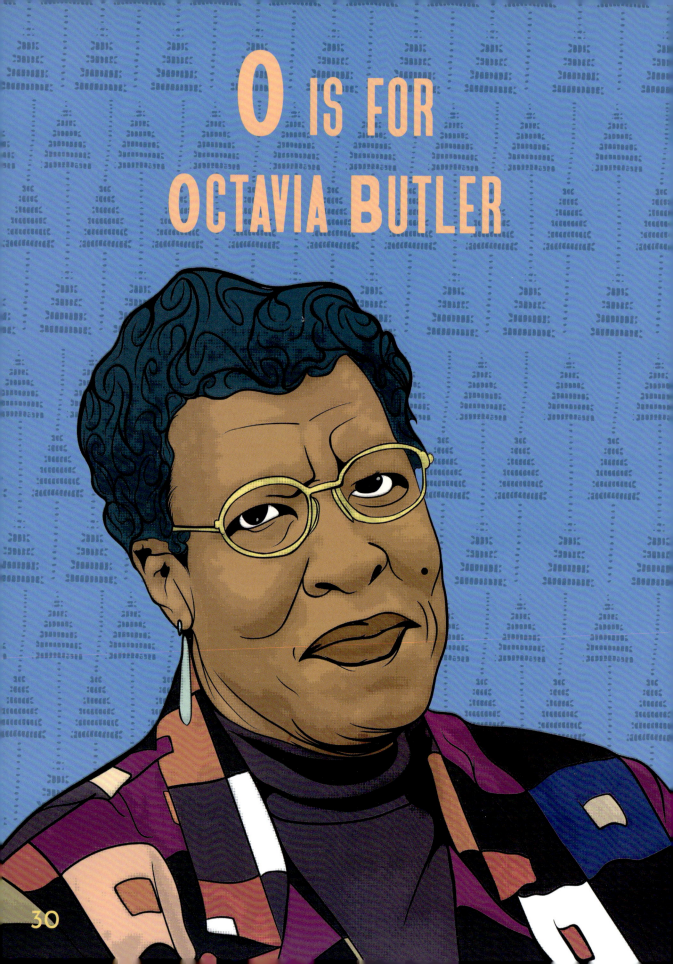

OCTAVIA BUTLER

WRITER. FEMINIST. TRUTH SPEAKER.

OCTAVIA SHARED HER BRILLIANCE WITH US THROUGH CREATIVE WRITING. AS ONE OF THE FIRST BLACK WOMEN TO PUBLISH SCIENCE FICTION BOOKS, SHE OPENED PEOPLE'S EYES TO THE IMPORTANCE OF INCLUDING DIVERSE PERSPECTIVES AND CHARACTERS. IN HER BOOKS, SHE USED FANTASY TO EXPLORE TOPICS LIKE PREJUDICE, HIERARCHY, RACE, FEMINISM, AND HUMANITY. HER WORK SPARKED A LITERARY MOVEMENT CALLED, AFROFUTURISM, AND SHE BECAME THE FIRST SCIENCE FICTION AUTHOR TO BE AWARDED THE MACARTHUR "GENIUS GRANT" FELLOWSHIP. OCTAVIA'S BRILLIANCE OPENED DOORS FOR OTHER GENERATIONS OF BLACK SCI-FI WRITERS THROUGH MENTORSHIP AND EDUCATION, AND HER STORIES STILL CAPTURE THE HEARTS AND MINDS OF SCIENCE FICTIONS LOVERS TO THIS DAY.

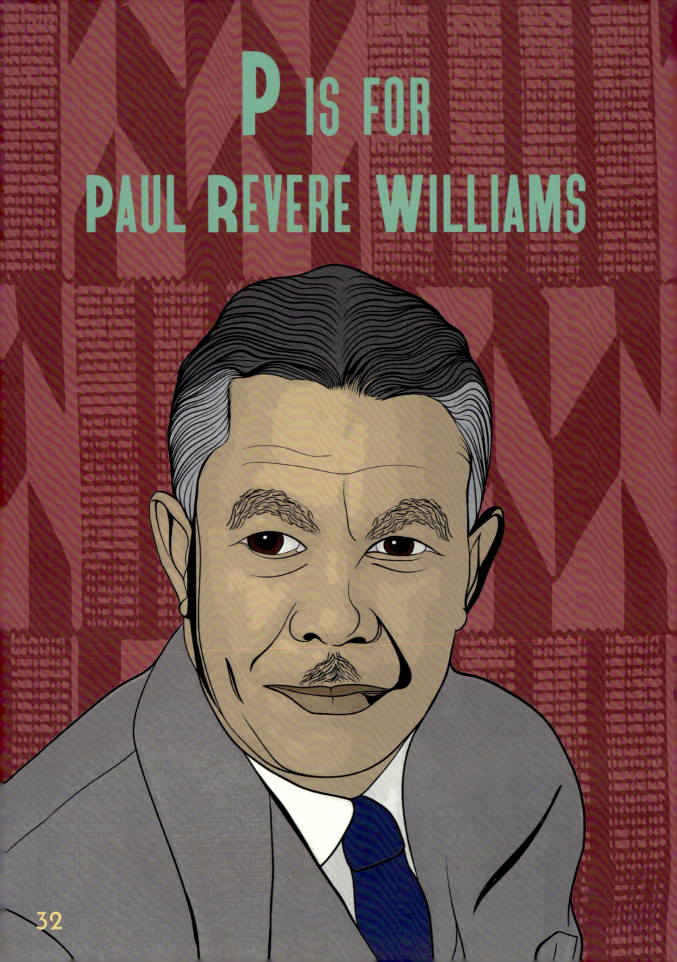

PAUL REVERE WILLIAMS

DESIGNER. ARCHITECT. ENTREPRENEUR.

PAUL SHARED HIS BRILLIANCE WITH US THROUGH DESIGN AND ARCHITECTURE. AS THE FIRST BLACK ARCHITECT TO PRACTICE ON THE WEST COAST, HE BECAME A MEMBER OF THE FIRST LOS ANGELES PLANNING COMMISSION. HE DESIGNED MORE THAN 2,000 PRIVATE HOMES IN THE HOLLYWOOD HILLS AND MID-WILSHIRE IN CALIFORNIA. HE DESIGNED HOMES FOR MANY CELEBRITIES INCLUDING BILL BOJANGLES ROBINSON AND LUCILLE BALL. HE ALSO DESIGNED HOUSING PROJECTS, CHURCHES, HOTELS, AND SCHOOLS. PAUL WORKED FOR THE NAVY DEPARTMENT DURING WWII AS AN ARCHITECT. PAUL CHALLENGED THE CONVENTIONS OF ARCHITECTURE IN THE UNITED STATES, AND HIS ELEGANT AND MODERN HOMES STILL SERVE AS MODELS OF EXCELLENCE AND QUALITY FOR MANY BLACK ARCHITECTS.

QUEEN LATIFAH

RAPPER. SINGER. GROUNDBREAKER.

QUEEN LATIFAH SHARES HER BRILLIANCE WITH US THROUGH HIP-HOP AND ENTERTAINMENT. SHE STARTED HER CAREER AS A FEMINIST RAPPER AND SINGER IN THE 1980S AND EARLY '90S. SHE WAS THE FIRST FEMALE HIP-HOP ARTIST TO BE NOMINATED FOR AN OSCAR AND THE FIRST HIP-HOP ARTIST TO RECEIVE A STAR ON THE HOLLYWOOD WALK OF FAME. HER LYRICS SPOKE ABOUT BEING A STRONG WOMAN. QUEEN LATIFAH HAS A TWO-OCTAVE VOCAL RANGE WHICH MAKES HER PERFORMANCES UNIQUE AND VIBRANT. QUEEN HAS ALSO ACTED IN AND PRODUCED MANY TV SHOWS, MOVIES, AND PLAYS. QUEEN LATIFAH CONTINUES TO REINVENT HERSELF AND SHOW YOUNGER GENERATIONS HOW HARD WORK AND DEDICATION TO YOUR CRAFT CAN OPEN DOORS FOR A LONG-LASTING ENTERTAINMENT CAREER.

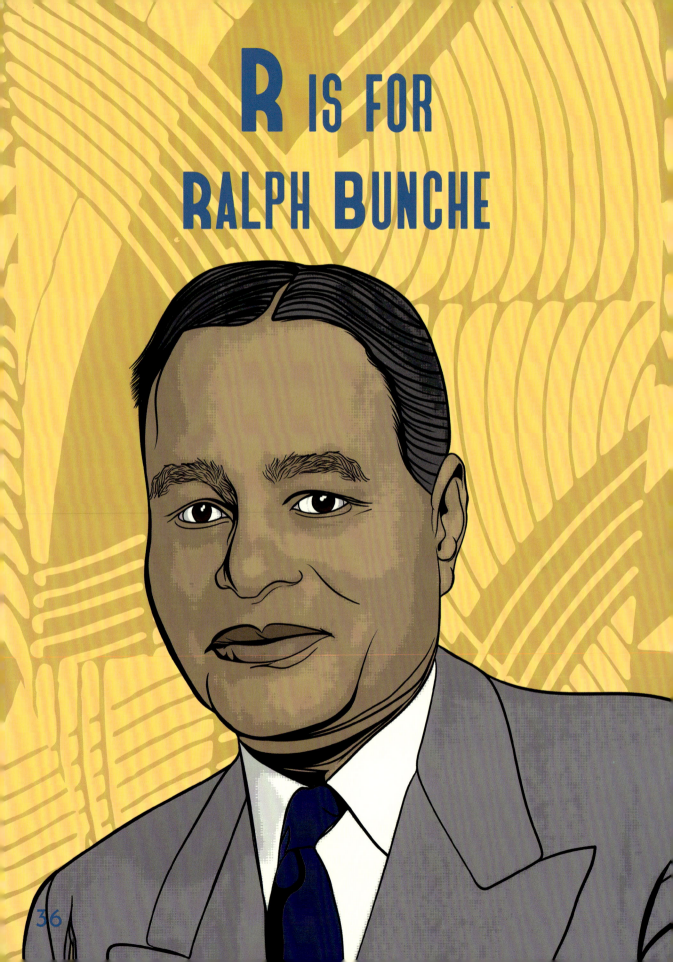

RALPH BUNCHE

DIPLOMAT. NOBEL LAUREATE. PEACEMAKER.

RALPH SHARED HIS BRILLIANCE WITH THE WORLD THROUGH FAIRNESS, PEACE, AND CREATIVE INNOVATION. HE WAS THE FIRST BLACK AMERICAN TO RECEIVE THE NOBEL PEACE PRIZE. HE RECEIVED THIS HONOR DURING HIS TIME AT THE UNITED NATIONS AS A RESULT OF SUCCESSFUL MEDIATIONS BETWEEN TWO DISAGREEING COUNTRIES. THESE CONVERSATIONS BROUGHT ELEMENTS OF PEACE TO THE TWO COUNTRIES. RALPH'S TECHNIQUES AND STRATEGIES FOR INTERNATIONAL PEACEKEEPING WERE SO EFFECTIVE THAT THEY ARE STILL USED TODAY. HE ALSO SUPPORTED THE 1960S CIVIL RIGHTS MOVEMENT AND SPOKE OUT AGAINST RACIAL INJUSTICE. RALPH'S VISION FOR PEACE STILL LIVES ON AT THE UNITED NATIONS AND OTHER GOVERNMENT AGENCIES.

"STAGECOACH" MARY FIELDS

MAIL CARRIER. MARKSWOMAN. BUSINESS OWNER.

"STAGECOACH" MARY SHARED HER BRILLIANCE WITH US THROUGH HER FEARLESSNESS AND RELIABILITY. SHE WAS THE FIRST BLACK WOMAN TO BECOME A STAR-ROUTE MAIL CARRIER. SHE BEGAN HER WORK AS A MAIL CARRIER AT THE AGE OF 60. HER ROUTE, THROUGH THE ROCKY TERRAIN OF MONTANA, WAS COLD AND TREACHEROUS FOR MOST OF THE YEAR. WITH HER FAMOUS STAGECOACH, HER SKILLS AS A MARKSWOMAN, AND HER PERSISTENCE, SHE NEVER MISSED A DAY OF MAIL DELIVERY. WHEN THE SNOW WAS TOO HIGH, SHE'D JUMP DOWN FROM HER STAGECOACH AND DELIVER THE MAIL ON FOOT. AFTER DELIVERING MAIL FOR 10 YEARS, SHE BABYSAT FOR HER FELLOW TOWNSPEOPLE AND OPENED A LAUNDROMAT. THE PEOPLE IN MARY'S TOWN LOVED HER SO MUCH THEY MADE HER BIRTHDAY AN OFFICIAL TOWN HOLIDAY. STAGECOACH MARY LEFT BEHIND A LEGACY OF FIERCENESS AND ENTREPRENEURSHIP THAT STILL SERVES AS A BENCHMARK FOR MANY BLACK BUSINESS OWNERS.

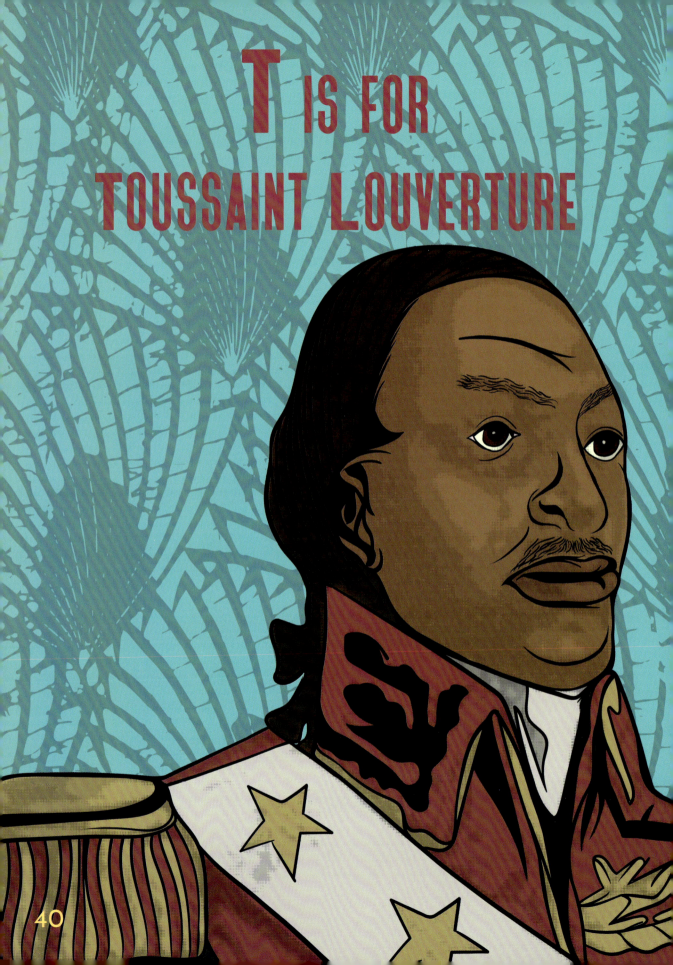

TOUSSAINT LOUVERTURE

ARMY GENERAL. NEGOTIATOR. POLITICIAN.

TOUSSAINT SHARED HIS BRILLIANCE WITH US THROUGH LEADERSHIP AND POLITICAL WISDOM. HE IS CONSIDERED THE MOST WELL-KNOWN LEADER OF THE HAITIAN REVOLUTION. HIS COMMITMENT TO ENDING ENSLAVEMENT IN HAITI CHANGED THE COURSE OF HISTORY. HE TURNED AN ENSLAVEMENT REBELLION INTO A FULL-FLEDGED REBELLION AGAINST THE FRENCH GOVERNMENT. HE WORKED TO IMPROVE HAITI'S WEALTH BY SECURING AGREEMENTS WITH THE UNITED KINGDOM AND THE UNITED STATES. HIS ACTS OF COURAGE AND BRAVERY HELPED HAITI TO BECOME A SOVEREIGN STATE. TOUSSAINT'S LEGACY LIVES ON TODAY, AND HE IS KNOWN AS THE "FATHER OF HAITI."

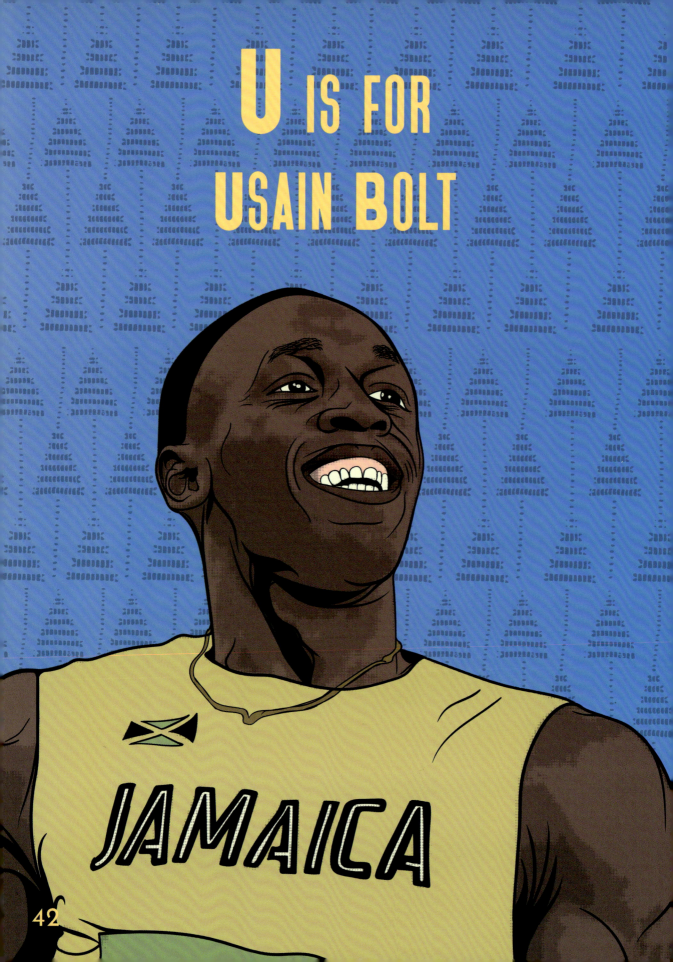

USAIN BOLT

SPRINTER. RECORD BREAKER. OLYMPIAN.

USAIN SHARES HIS BRILLIANCE WITH US THROUGH ATHLETICISM, DISCIPLINE, AND PRIDE. HE IS CONSIDERED ONE OF THE GREATEST SPRINTERS OF ALL TIME AND HAS BEEN GIVEN THE NICKNAME "LIGHTING BOLT." IN THE SPORT OF TRACK AND FIELD, HE HOLDS 3 WORLD RECORDS AND HAS 8 OLYMPIC GOLD MEDALS. HE IS ALSO THE FIRST ATHLETE TO WIN 4 WORLD CHAMPIONSHIP TITLES IN THE 200 METER RACE. IN ADDITION TO HIS ATHLETIC ACCOMPLISHMENTS, HE COFOUNDED A COMPANY THAT CREATES MOBILITY DEVICES AND HAS BECOME A MUSIC PRODUCER. USAIN HAS BECOME TRACK AND FIELD'S MOST RECOGNIZABLE ATHLETE AND HAS HELPED CHANGED THE FUTURE OF MARKETING AND BRANDING FOR THE YOUNGER ATHLETES WHO WANT TO FOLLOW IN HIS RUNNING SHOES.

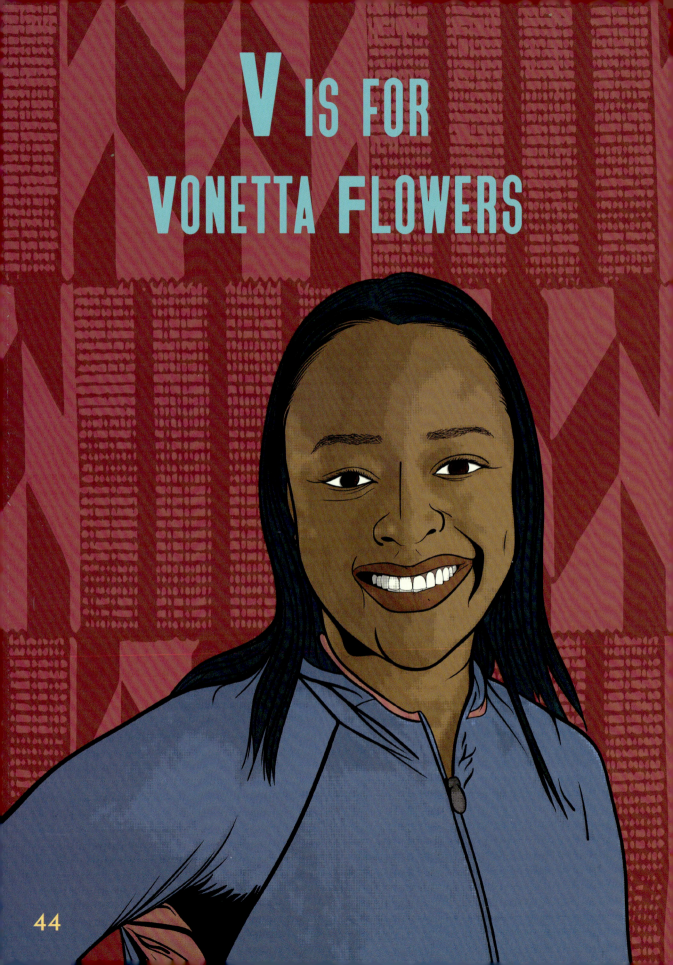

VONETTA FLOWERS

BOBSLEDDER. GROUNDBREAKER. OLYMPIAN.

VONETTA SHARES HER BRILLIANCE WITH US THROUGH PERSEVERANCE AND FAITH. VONETTA STARTED HER ATHLETIC CAREER AS A SPRINTER. SHE TRIED TO QUALIFY FOR THE SUMMER OLYMPICS A FEW TIMES BUT DID NOT SECURE A SPOT. SHE CHANGED HER FOCUS AND JOINED THE UNITED STATES BOBSLEDDING TEAM. VONETTA FLOWERS BECAME THE FIRST BLACK WOMAN FROM ANY COUNTRY TO WIN A GOLD MEDAL IN THE WINTER OLYMPICS. VONETTA WAS SELECTED TO JOIN THE ALABAMA SPORTS HALL OF FAME AND WAS INDUCTED IN 2011. VONETTA'S HARD WORK AS AN ATHLETE SHOWS PEOPLE WHAT IS POSSIBLE WHEN THEY HAVE FAITH AND BELIEVE IN THEMSELVES.

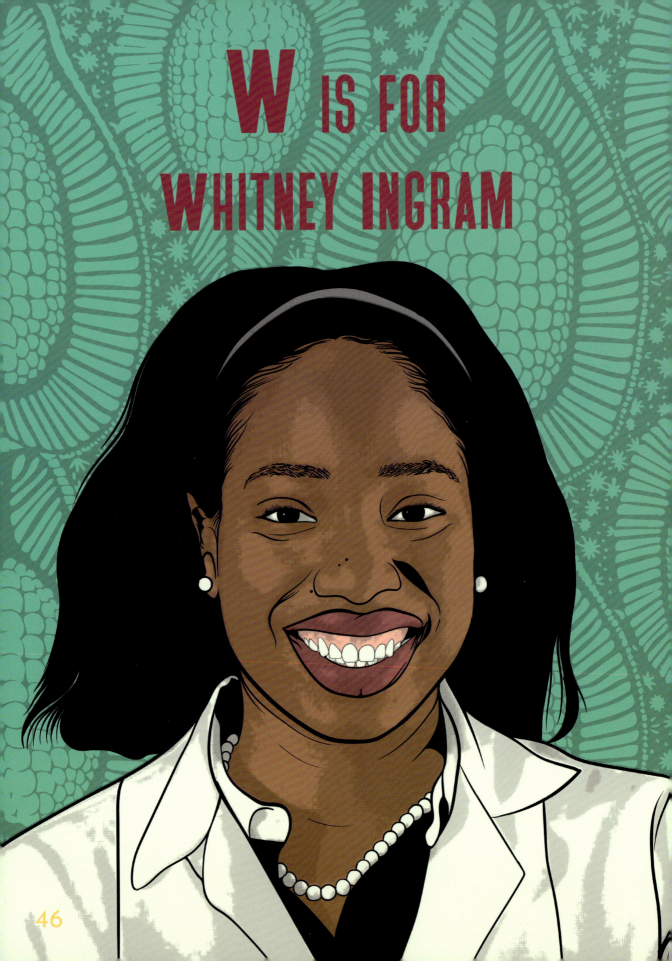

WHITNEY INGRAM

PHD. PIONEER. SCIENTIST.

WHITNEY SHARES HER BRILLIANCE WITH US THROUGH SCIENCE AND EDUCATION. SHE IS THE FIRST BLACK WOMAN TO GRADUATE WITH A PHD IN PHYSICS FROM THE UNIVERSITY OF GEORGIA. SHE FOCUSES ON DESIGNING AND BUILDING NANOTECHNOLOGY. SHE IS 1 OF ONLY 100 WOMEN IN THE US WHO HAVE A PHD IN PHYSICS. SHE ACTIVELY SUPPORTS MORE WOMEN ENTERING INTO THE FIELD OF PHYSICS. WHITNEY INGRAM CURRENTLY WORKS IN A LABORATORY AND HOPES TO ONE DAY SHARE HER KNOWLEDGE WITH HER STUDENTS AS A PHYSICS PROFESSOR. WHITNEY'S ACHIEVEMENTS SHOW OTHER BLACK STUDENTS THAT IT'S POSSIBLE TO REACH FOR THE STARS AND BEYOND WHEN IT COMES TO EXCELLING IN ACADEMIA.

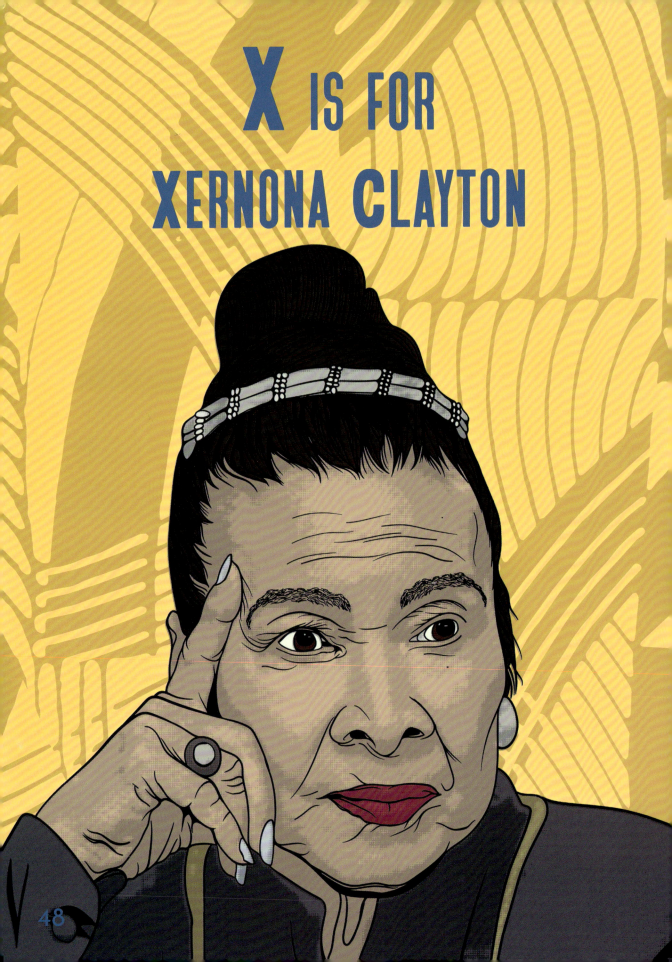

XERNONA CLAYTON

EDUCATOR. SISTER. PHILANTHROPIST.

XERNONA SHARES HER BRILLIANCE WITH US THROUGH SEEKING THE TRUTH AND COMMUNICATION. SHE WAS AN ACTIVE 1960S CIVIL RIGHTS LEADER WHO INVESTIGATED EMPLOYMENT DISCRIMINATION. SHE ALSO HELPED PLAN AND ORGANIZE DR. MARTIN LUTHER KING'S MARCHES. SHE BECAME THE FIRST BLACK WOMAN TO HOST A DAILY PRIME TIME TALK SHOW IN ATLANTA AND SERVED AS AN EXECUTIVE AT TURNER BROADCASTING. XERNONA CLAYTON STILL USES HER VOICE TO ADVOCATE FOR CIVIL RIGHTS, AND SHE ALSO SERVES ON THE BOARD OF DIRECTORS FOR THE KING CENTER FOR NONVIOLENT SOCIAL CHANGE.

YAA ASANTEWAA

QUEEN. WARRIOR. CATALYST.

YAA SHARED HER BRILLIANCE WITH US THROUGH PRIDE AND BRAVERY. SHE WAS THE QUEEN MOTHER OF EJISU IN THE ASHANTI EMPIRE. AS QUEEN MOTHER SHE LED AN ARMY OF OVER 5,000 ASANTE PEOPLE TO FIGHT AGAINST BRITISH COLONIALISM. SHE WAS THE FIRST AND ONLY WOMAN TO LEAD THE ASANTE FIGHTING FORCE. YAA ASANTEWAA IS STILL SEEN AS A BRILLIANT FEMALE LEADER AND INTEGRAL PART OF ASANTE AND GHANA HISTORY.

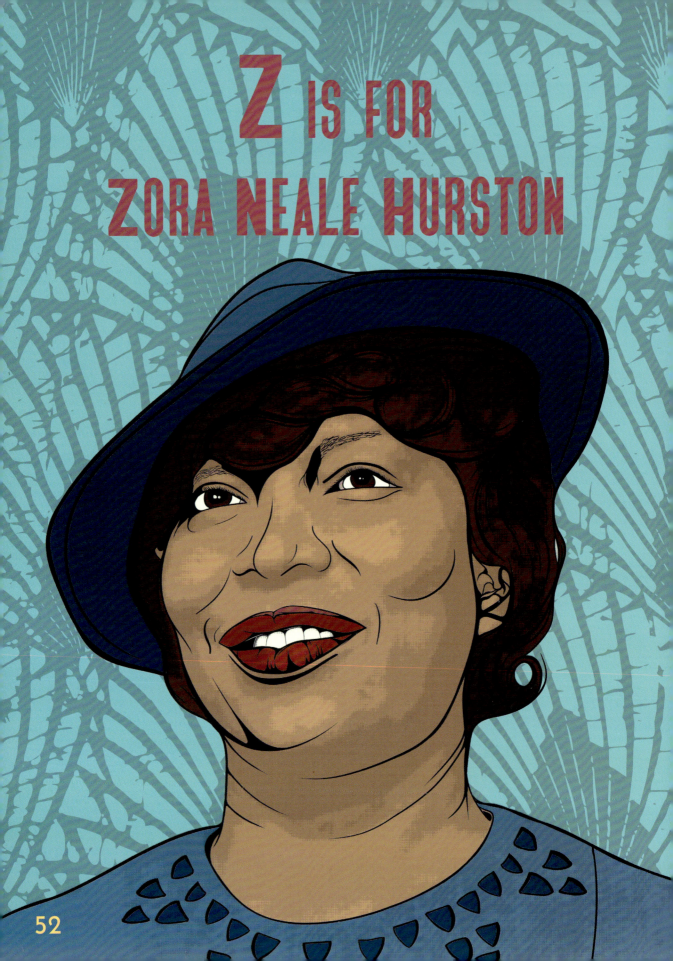

ZORA NEALE HURSTON

ANTHROPOLOGIST. WRITER. VISIONARY.

ZORA SHARED HER BRILLIANCE WITH THE WORLD THROUGH LITERATURE AND ANTHROPOLOGICAL STUDIES. HAVING GROWN UP IN EATONVILLE, THE FIRST BLACK FOUNDED AND INCORPORATED TOWN IN AMERICA, ZORA SAW AND EXPERIENCED A COMMUNITY FOUNDED ON BLACK EMPOWERMENT. THROUGHOUT HER LIFE, SHE TRAVELED THE WORLD TO STUDY AND PROMOTE BLACK CULTURE AND BLACK BRILLIANCE. SHE WAS AT THE CENTER OF THE HARLEM RENAISSANCE, PRODUCING THE LITERARY MAGAZINE, "FIRE", THAT SHOWCASED MANY YOUNG, BLACK ARTISTS AND WRITERS. ZORA'S WORK GAVE US INSIGHT INTO THE EXPERIENCE OF ENSLAVED PEOPLE AND AFRICAN AMERICAN FOLKTALES AND TRADITIONS. HER WORK CONNECTS US TO THE LIVES OF OUR ANCESTORS AND SHARES MANY UNTOLD STORIES THAT SHOW THE PARALLELS OF THE BLACK EXPERIENCE THEN AND NOW.

JOIN THE B IS FOR BLACK BRILLIANCE MOVEMENT

Facebook: www.facebook.com/bisforblackbrilliance
Instagram: @bisforblackbrilliance
Web: www.bisforblackbrilliance.com

If you bought this book at an online bookstore, please take a moment to review us!

AUTHOR AND ILLUSTRATOR

SHAWNA WELLS is the author of *B is for Black Brilliance*. Shawna is an advocate for young Black children and their ability to lead lives of abundance and liberation through quality learning experiences and education. During her childhood, she noticed an absence of Black brilliance and contributions in school material, television programs, and public places. That realization inspired Shawna's personal mission to change the narrative on how the world is educated about Black brilliance and Black people's integral contributions to mainstream society.

Shawna's deep respect for learning, diversity, and inclusion led her on a journey to establish a school in West Philadelphia and a coaching practice for Black senior leaders to have excellent support in order to thrive in their professional roles.

Shawna has taken her years of professional experience to launch the *B is for Black Brilliance Company* where the collective goal is to create a world where Black brilliance is widely acknowledged and celebrated. When Shawna is not busy pioneering for various educational causes, she can be found spending quality time with her family or gardening.

KELLIE MARSH is the visual artist and founder of London based company "KDM Graphic Design LTD." He is an avid and experienced graphic designer and illustrator with many years industry experience operating as a freelance artist and designer.

With great passion for illustration, Kellie blends the digital art, traditional art and graphic design worlds to produce visually appealing and creative pieces.

ACKNOWLEDGEMENTS

At *B is for Black Brilliance* we believe in the power of gratitude. Gratitude is the driving force behind our movement and gave us the courage to write our book. In honor of our first book release and the launch of our movement, we want to take a moment to share our gratitude with the universe:

- To our ancestors, especially Willie Pearl Wells, for their unwavering support and energy throughout this process

- To our families and friends who nourish our souls and give us the confidence to take big leaps of faith

- To Gabrielle Wyatt at The Highland Project for giving us inspiration

- To Kim Griffith for her generosity, enthusiasm, and connectivity

- To Meisha Mayo at *Pen2Paper* Editorial for breathing energy into our words

- To Carmen Stacey at Stay Carm for giving us beautiful imagery to help our concept come to life

- To our 258 Kickstarter supporters whose generosity helped bring our vision to print

- To YOU for spreading the word about our book and our movement

We can't thank you enough!